D1597823

VANISHING GWINNETT

Photos for this book came from various sources,
as marked. Those labeled GWN are from the
Vanishing Georgia Collection of the Georgia
Department of Archives and History from whom
prints can be ordered. Their address is
330 Capitol Ave., Atlanta, GA 30334

Identification of dust jacket
photograph may be found on
pages 14 and 15.

VANISHING GWINNETT

GWINNETT COUNTY, GEORGIA

Pictorial History of Bygone Days

by
W. Dorsey Stancil

assisted by
Alice Smythe McCabe, John J. Hood,
John W. Baughman, Jr., Elliott Brack
and Robert E. Wynn

Gwinnett Historical Society, Inc.
P.O. Box 261
Lawrenceville, Georgia 30246

Copies of this book may be purchased from

Gwinnett Historical Society
P.O. Box 261
Lawrenceville, GA 30246

CONTENTS

ACKNOWLEDGMENTS

Many have contributed their time, energies, ideas, experience and talents to this book and we appreciate them all.

First, we thank the Georgia Department of Archives and History and particularly their former director, Miss Carroll Hart, whose dreams became reality in their *Vanishing Georgia* slide collection and book. We want to thank all those who submitted Gwinnett County photos to that project enabling us to have a good selection for this book. Thanks go to others who brought or mailed photos to our office and who helped identify pictures for us. We appreciate the courier service of Diane Coleman of the *Gwinnett Daily News* as well as that paper's editorial support and editor Bob Wynn's careful historical editing. We thank too, the *Gwinnett Extra* and *Lawrenceville Home Weekly* papers for their publicity. Mildred Breedlove and Lamar Cooper typed copy for the book and John McCabe and Jean Todd helped proof read.

The Harrison Company, Publishers, Norcross deserves our rich appreciation for the donation of the services of their typographer, Donna Helms, and the typesetting for this publication.

We thank all who purchased the book in advance and those who will buy it when it is completed.

We thank the following who offered identification help and photos whether or not they were used: Stanley Allen, Mildred Amos, Geraldine Arnold, Lucile Baldwin, Catherine Banks, Louise Barbee, John W. Baughman, Jr., Ben Baxter, Sim Bennett, Tillie Bolton, Stella Bowen, G. S. Bowman, Lorraine Brock, Margie Brogdon, Bessie Briscoe, Marion Britt, Lowell Browning, Mae Burge, Louise Burton, Billy Cain, Lillie Caldwell (deceased), Eugene Chatham, Dorothy Clack, Hazel S. Clower, Dick Corbin, Minor M. Corley, Nancy Cornell, Mary Claire Cox, Daisy Craig, Curtis Cooper, James H. Dempsey, Fraser Duke, Douglas Eason, Annie Frances Flanigan, Carolyn Foreman (deceased), Mildred Fort, Herman Fowler, Wendell and Elizabeth Fuller, Delia Gilliland, Betty Jo Givens, Edith Green, Evelyn Green, Dora Gunter, Maude P. Hamilton, Thelma Hendricks, Rosie Higgins, Edna G. Hood, John and Tommye Hood, Barbara Howington, Arnold Huff, Helen Hutchens, Frances Johnson, Sam Johnson,

Sarah Johnson, Beulah Jones, Claud H. Jordan, Mary Alice Juhan, Helen M. Kirby, Fannie Knight, Lawrenceville Woman's Club, Ann Lynn Link, Larry Mabrey, Dave Magoon, Mildred Martin, Bill Maughon, Evelyn Mays, Horace E. McAdams, Alice McCabe, Mrs. _____ McCullough, Randy Moore, Laura Morton, Ruby W. Ogletree, Lizzie N. Peevy, Charles L. Pentecost, Lyman H. Phillips, Martha Phillips, Joyce Pickens, Davis Pierce, Lula Pirkle, Pauline Pounds, Brenda Pruitt, Crawford Puckett, Alice H. Ray, Margaret Ritchie, Loretta Roberts, Virginia Roberts, Carrie F. Russell, Mr. and Mrs. Robert F. Saine, Janis Sawyer, Jeannette Sears, Golden Shadburn, Harold Simonton, Nolan D. Singleton, Codell Skelton, Wayne and Clara Stancel, S. W. Stancel, Cline Stancel, W. Dorsey Stancil, Margaret Tanner, W. 0. Thompson, Jr., Hoyt Tuggle, H. Spurgeon Tullis, Perrin and Inez Walker, Lucy Wallis, Emory White, Thelma Whiting, Mary Ellen Williams, Joy Woodall, Robert E. Wynn

INTRODUCTION

Ever since we of the Gwinnett Historical Society first heard of the *Vanishing Georgia* project of the Georgia Department of Archives and History, we have been enthusiastic about having a book of photos of bygone days in Gwinnett County. When the *Vanishing Georgia* book came out, we were positive that we wanted to produce one, too. Because theirs was such a beautiful volume, we decided to ride on their successful coattails and make ours a companion piece that would, we hope, grace every coffee table in Gwinnett County.

The book is divided into sections depicting various aspects of life in the county with emphasis on events and buildings that no longer exist. Of course, we could not use all the pictures that were offered, although we would have liked to, but we had to keep the cost within reason.

An index of individual names is followed by one for subjects mentioned herein. In long lists, we sometimes used a blank instead of a name and we hope that readers will be able to fill in those blanks for us.

We hope this book will stir up memories in the old and whet the appetites of the young for more stories of days past.

Alice Smythe McCabe
Project Manager

PREFACE

There are photographs of the 1850s and Matthew Brady became famous for his photography in the era of the War Between the States. But it was not until the 1880s that photography came into its own. It is, therefore, from that period forward that we drew the bulk of our collection.

The credit for the majority of the photographs in this book must go to the Vanishing Georgia Project of the Georgia Department of Archives and History, and those pictures marked with a GWN number indicate the archives' file number for each photograph. Additional photos were submitted by others and those are credited to the lender, instead of Archives GWN numbers.

Other abbreviations used are m. for married and GHS for Gwinnett Historical Society.

Photos used in *Vanishing Georgia* book or in earlier publications of Gwinnett Historical Society are not repeated in this book.

Much effort has gone into identifying individuals pictured and in dating buildings and scenes. Wherever possible, the present 1984 location was given, which is in itself a historical record for future readers. Our listing of people in groups is incomplete and we offer our apologies and ask that readers continue our work by telling us of errors and omissions by contacting the office of the Gwinnett Historical Society.

Lastly, we hope that you enjoy *VANISHING GWINNETT* and derive some of the pleasure that we have had in producing it. The pictures are fascinating and they have a subtle way of continuing to show something new at every glance.

Buford, Georgia   W. Dorsey Stancil
1 August, 1984   Author

VANISHING GWINNETT

THE GOVERNMENT

Gwinnett County was created on December 15, 1818 by an act of the Georgia Legislature of the Capital in Milledgeville, from Cherokee lands and from a part of Jackson County.

In 1914 a portion of Gwinnett vanished from our tax rolls when Barrow County was created out of Gwinnett, Hall, and Jackson Counties. In the mid 1950s more land vanished, quite literally, as the Chattahoochee River backed up behind Buford Dam and hundreds of acres were covered by the waters of Lake Lanier.

The home of Elisha Winn in Hog Mountain was selected as the first center of government of the new county and the first elections were held there. The first jail was located adjacent to his huge barn that doubled as the first courtroom. In 1820, a temporary log courthouse was built by Isham Williams on Land Lot 143 near what would become Lawrenceville at a cost of $56 but failure to agree on a purchase price for the land brought another move when Elisha Winn purchased 250 acres in land lot 146 for $200 from John Breedlove. A second temporary log courthouse was built in what became Lawrenceville to serve until the first permanent courthouse was completed in 1824. This building, costing $4000, burned along with many records in 1871. A second permanent courthouse was built on the square in 1872 but it proved to be so thoroughly inadequate that it was torn down in 1884 and replaced in 1885 with the building which became known as the Old Courthouse that served until the opening of the Justice and Administration Center. No known photograph exists of any of these buildings except the Winn House, the Old Courthouse, and the Justice and Administration Center.

The growth of the county and the subsequent creation of towns brought about the need for law enforcement facilities, firemen, utilities, post offices, and the many facets of organized government at the county, state, and national levels.

Elisha Winn House built c. 1812.
(*Photo by Frances Johnson*)

The courthouse in 1907, *right,* looked much as it did when constructed in 1885 at a cost of $23,083. *(GWN 242)*

The clock tower, *left,* was added in 1908 for $4,000, and featured decorative urns, balconies, pediments, and Corinthian pilasters, all made of pressed metal. The building was enlarged on the Pike Street side in 1935 for $8,000-10,000. *(GHS Collection)*

Neighbors grade Singleton Road in Berkshire District in 1920. Land owners had the option of paying road tax or doing the work themselves. Pictured here are Will McDaniel (seated behind scrape), Will Singleton (far right) and, next to him, (on horse) Cliff Singleton. *(Photo from Delia Gilliland)*

The old jail facing Perry Street at Luckie Street, Lawrenceville, in 1953. The sheriff and family once lived in three rooms downstairs, using them for kitchen, living and dining rooms, and upstairs, they had one bedroom with two women's cells behind. Male prisoners were on the first floor. The basement had a boiler room and storage for contraband, such as liquor and slot machines. Crawford Pittard (term 1953-60) was the last sheriff to live here. The jail was demolished in 1978 and a new Fire Station built there in 1980. *(GHS Collection)*

Two hangings in Lawrenceville, one legal and one a lynching. Charlie Hale, *left*, a black man, was lynched on the courthouse square, corner Perry and Pike, April 7, 1911. The sign hanging from his toes is inscribed, "Please do not wake him." Jack Mathis is at far left; the boy is Herbert Strayhorn. *(GWN 277)*

Opposite page Henry Campbell was hanged in Lawrenceville May 8, 1908, after his trial and conviction for the murder of Ella Hudson and her four-month-old daughter. He earlier had addressed the crowd of spectators, stating that an innocent man was going to his death. *(Photo from Randy Moore)*

Left, Governor John M. Slayton is hung in effigy in downtown Dacula, June, 1915; building at right was medical office of Dr. Sam Hinton and later became the Dacula Post Office. The placard beneath the dummy reads, "GOVERNOR JOHN M SLAYTON THE KING OF JEWS". The governor had just commuted the death sentence of Leo M. Frank to life imprisonment. Frank, convicted of the murder of Mary Phagan in Atlanta, was later taken from the prison in Milledgeville and carried to Marietta and lynched. Public opinion against the governor was so great that he and his family fled the state.*(GWN 150)*

Suffragettes, *right,* demonstrate in Dacula for passage of the 19th Amendment to the U. S. Constitution, permitting women to vote. The efforts of the suffragette movement were successful in 1920. *(GWN 151B)*

11

Some of the first county draftees for World War I wait in the shade of the bandstand on the southwest corner of the courthouse square in 1917 for a bus to carry them to fight in "the war to end all wars." *Left to right*, seated: Clyde Y. Nix, Chalmers Powell, Robert Vance, Athel Garner; standing: Frank Robinson, Carl Nix, Leonard Hinton, Kelley Alford, Hugh Garner, Roland Moore, and Ben Shackelford. (*GWN 216*)

Confederate veterans unite for their last local reunion on the west side of the courthouse in 1912. Front row: Maj. W. E. Simmons, Col. Sam J. Winn, Andrew Garner, Dick Mills, Nathan Bulloch, _____, _____, Dr. T. K. Mitchell, _____, Jim Whitworth, James M. Singleton, Rev. W. L. Singleton, Samuel A. Edmonds, William J. Turner, John McDaniel, Cyrenus Summerlin, Hiram Etheridge, _____, Isham W. Bennett, Taylor Benjamin Cook. 2nd row: _____, Washington N. Franklin, _____, _____, Eli Cornelius McDaniel, Jacob C. Lowery, _____, _____, Archibald Holland, A. M. Baxter, Sam Jones Ewing, _____, Wilson L. Vaughn, Max Waits, _____, _____, _____, _____. 3rd row: Elijah Casey, _____, John W. Cates, Stephen T. McElroy, George Washington Mills, _____, George W. Hopkins, (9 unknown), Robert McDaniel, _____. 4th row: Daniel M. Clower, _____, George W. Sims, Wm. Henry Sudderth, _____, _____, _____, _____, _____, Judge John Webb, _____, _____, _____, _____, J. P. Biggers, _____, _____, _____, _____, _____. Names furnished by Charles Pentecost. (*GWN 320*)

Lawrenceville's fire department was officially organized on September 15, 1912. In late 1912 or early 1913, proud city fathers, firemen, and the new fire equipment were posed for this photograph which showed the Ezzard-Montgomery Drug Co., later becoming Monfort Drugs, the courthouse, and the Cornett Hotel in the background: In the first horse-drawn fire carriage, *left to right*: Charlie McConnell, Lawrence Exum, John Langley, Clint Shackelford, William A. Roberts, and Quillian (Dock) Comfort. Seated in the second horse-drawn wagon, *left to right*: Lum Brown, Cleveland Mason, Pascall Boyce, Charlie H. Roberts, Joe Davis, and Charlie McKelvey.

14

Standing in front of hotel, *left to right*: Policeman Tom Davis, City Attorney Dan M. Byrd, City Councilmen: Lenton Ewing, and John P. Webb, Mayor Lovick R. Martin, City Councilmen: J. H. McGee, and John H. Britt, Policeman Bob Wages. On horse cart, *left to right*: John Garner, _____Pye, F. B. Dobb, J. C. Oakes, Victor Hutchins, Willis Holland, Leon Wallace, and Fred Byrd. Not shown here but seen on the dust jacket of this book, *far left*: Otis Kelley drives new 1913 Rambler automobile carrying Bob Sammon and Fire Chief Frank Taylor. (This and dust jacket photo from Robert E. (Bob) Wynn. Also, in order, GWN 270, 268, 297, and 269)

15

Thirty-four years separate these two views of the Buford Fire Department. *Left*, They pose with their new 1925 American LaFrance fire truck in front of the new City Hall. Standing, *left to right*, Policeman Ernest Murphy, _____, _____, Johnny Crescenti, Sr. (on wheel), Ed Roper (far right). Next row behind, *left to right*, Clyde W. Davis (on truck), Anse Forrester (at wheel), Logan Kelley, Townsend Parker, Roy King (with dog), _____, Thesta Settle. (GWN 136)

Right: Buford Volunteer Firemen and City Commissioners pose in front of the 1959 Ford American LaFrance fire truck. *Left to right*: kneeling: Chief Buddy Ehlert, Ryman Higgins, David House, John Henry Maddox, James Wilson. Standing: Stanley Allen, Millard Peevy, Howard Stephens, Wendall Dean, Jay Wiley, Samuel Stancel, Harold Bagwell, Otto Whitley, George Mathis, Richard Wilson, Early Biffle, and Loss Sears. In the background is the 1946 Post Office which became the City Hall when the post office moved to a new location on Buford Highway at Church Street. Columns and cupola, marble floors and wainscotting and wooden paneling, found in this building, are things of the past. Today, public buildings stress stark modernity and utilitarianism. (*GWN 151*)

Snellville district courthouse built c. 1880 at the corner of Pate Road and present U. S. 78 is now demolished. (GWN 199)

In 1911, a patron enters the Norcross Post Office, located on South Peachtree Road. The Post Office relocated in 1958 to the corner of Thrasher and Jones streets, the site of the old Brunswick Hotel. (*GWN 252*)

ON THE FARM

Agriculture has been the principal industry in Gwinnett through most of its 166 years as it was in all Georgia. Eli Whitney's invention of the cotton gin outside of Savannah in 1793 made upland cotton a profitable commodity, and within a generation of this invention, cotton became the chief crop of the South and was referred to as "King Cotton".

Georgia's most productive year for cotton was 1913 when the state's largest percentage of population lived on farms. The decade from 1910 to 1920 was an era of high prices for farm products; farmers expanded their arable lands, sometimes planting crops right up to the front yards. The "boll weevil depression" from 1920 to 1923 was caused by both the attack of the boll weevil insect and the glut of cotton caused by overproduction. By 1932 the price paid for cotton had fallen to five cents per pound and the Great Depression was in full force. Although it would be planted in the county for two more decades, the death knell had been sounded for "King Cotton".

Contour plowing, introduced in the 1840s was adopted by Gwinnett farmers. The rolling farmlands were terraced and rows curved around the contours of the land preventing the rich soil's erosion. In the 1930s kudzu was touted as a valuable soil-binder and source of fodder for feeding cattle, and farmers were encouraged to plant kudzu on the terrace rows. It grew out of bounds when farmlands went out of cultivation and abandoned houses and barns, fields, forests, and utility poles have vanished beneath the rampant vines.

Hogs, cattle, and goats were widely raised here, although mostly for domestic use. Many farmers had routes in towns where they sold their milk, butter, and eggs, and many stores accepted these products in exchange for other goods. Winter was the time of hog killing after the hogs had been fattened over the summer. The hams and other cuts of meat were buried under salt in the salt box and the fatty parts were cooked in iron wash pots with the fat rendering down to lard and the meat becoming cracklings. Cracklings were ground and added to cornbread making a delicious crackling bread. Smaller cuts of meat were ground into sausage with sage and pepper added. The brains were a delicacy as were the lights, otherwise known as

Harvest time in 1908 at the home of William Thompson Britt between Oak Road and present U. S. 78 on Highpoint Road in Snellville. Child with doll is Connie Britt; William Britt *(left)* by horse drawn buggy, and his son, Clifford Hugh Britt, *(right)* sits on horse-drawn corn and cotton stalk cutter, and Mrs. Ida Johnson Britt draws water from the well. House burned *c.* 1960. Apartments cover the location today. *(Photo from Hazel Mitchell).*

lungs. Various parts of scrap meat were ground together with spices and served as pressed meat.

The 1950s saw the zenith of the poultry industry, and Gainesville to the north of the county in Hall County became known as the Poultry Capital of the World. The farmers of Gwinnett entered into the meteoric industry of growing broilers. In 1950, sixty three million broilers were produced in the state, an increase of 125 percent over the 1935 number. By 1961 the price of undressed poultry dropped to eleven cents per pound, a serious drop in the industry, causing many a farmer to abandon his chicken house. Subdivisions sprout and spread today on the former farmlands.

Howard Huff farm in 1920s on present
State Road 120 between Duluth and
Lawrenceville. *(GWN 336)*

J. C. Allen, a photographer from West Lafayette, Indiana, caught Sim Bennett picking cotton in fall, 1927. Mr. Allen was touring the south seeking photographs for the cover of magazine, "THE PROGRESSIVE FARMER". The house in the background became site of businesses on U. S. 78 west of Snellville. Mr. Bennett personalized his hamper basket and his picksack with his name written with poke berries. (*Photo from Sim Bennett*)

Facing: Inzie Stancel (m. Herman Gower) catches her brothers, sisters and parents on film in 1930 at Duncan Creek. *Left to right*, front: Herman, Sarah (m. James T. Boggs), Bonnie (m. Byron Cleghorn), and Cline. Back row, *left to right*: cousin, Audrey Hays (m. Thurman Collins), Lennie (m. Lester S. Maddox), J. T. with hamper basket, Mrs. Nora Hays Stancel, Mr. Walter Stancel, Samuel and Gladston. (*Photo from Cline Stancel*)

Emory Anderson Montgomery and Jess Masters with a pea thrasher near Union Grove Church. This apparatus was driven by a gasoline engine which beat dried pea pods, breaking them open. The peas fell into a hopper and the hulls were discarded or used for animal feed. This type machine is supposed to have made a horrible racket. (*Photo from Steve Montgomery*)

Opposite Mrs. Julie Stapp milks the family cow while her husband, John, waves a stick with a rag attached to shoo away the flies that would bite the cow, making her kick and swish her tail. Their farm was on Beaver Ruin Road near Norcross at a location now occupied by commercial development. The name of the cow has not come down to us. (*Photo from Tillie Bolton*)

Left Oxen pull a load for Mr. David Lockridge near Suwanee. (*GWN 131*)

Opposite Harvesting of rye and wheat fields for straw used in the Allen factory for horse collar stuffing. This was in the hundred acre field at present intersection of Buford Highway and Lee Street in Buford in the 1920s. Children in foreground earned money by selling rabbits in town that they had caught in the mown fields. (*GWN 357*)

James M. Fowler and son, James Floyd Fowler, use two-horse mowing machine in 1946 on Frank Wood farm, Dacula. *(Photo from Herman Fowler)*

John Henry Johnson plows on John Moore homeplace on Suwanee-Lawrenceville Road near McKendree Church in 1943. Mr. Johnson was well known in Lawrenceville where he peddled watermelons in summer and made ax handles and sold them to the county for the convicts to use in roadwork. (*Photo from Dorothy Clack*)

Left: Mrs. Mattie Puckett feeds her hens on Braselton Highway, Hog Mountain, in the 1930s. *(GWN 99)*

In the harvest fields of Arthur Brogdon,
Buford, *c.* 1910. *(GWN 179)*

Mr. and Mrs. Homer Tuggle show their enormous collard plant grown c. 1951. (*Photo from Billy Cain*)

Opposite The Billy Pickens family pose c. 1889-90 in front of their log barn, previously their home in which some of them were born. *Left to right*: Joe Pickens, John Pickens, Plennie Pickens, Sallie Pickens, Aunt "Bet" Pickens, Lou Pickens, and Billy Pickens. Homestead was near what became U. S. 29 in Lilburn. (*GWN 84*)

Kate Maltbie Terrell and Clara Rowland Terrell *c.* 1910 feed turkeys at their birthplace, the Kenan Terrell home. They never married and they died at home. They were the children of Kenan Troup Terrell II and Maria Judith Terrell. *(GWN 346)*

Opposite Fletcher Puckett was caught by a photographer near Auburn in 1918 with three vanishing subjects: the farm, the horse and buggy, and the outhouse. *(GWN 104)*

AT HOME

The first homes built in newly-created Gwinnett were mostly of logs, as were the barns and outbuildings. A family might abandon their first rude home in favor of a more substantial one, or they might improve on the original house. Often, as the family fortunes increased, so did the house: Log walls were veneered in weatherboarding and wooden shutters gave way to glass windows. Growing families dictated the need for more space and the original house might be expanded again and again.

Large sheets of glass were once unobtainable; therefore window panes were necessarily small. Double-hung windows were known by the number of panes in a sash; 6 over 9 meant six panes in the upper sash and nine in the lower. By the last third of the 1800s, some homes had the more expensive full-paned windows. A frugal housebuilder might put large pane windows in front and smaller ones on the sides and rear. Because blue light was considered healthful, colored glass often bordered windows and doors.

Porches were considered a necessity and came in many forms. The back porch was a place to stack firewood and store everyday essentials. The front porch was often furnished with chairs, rockers and porch swings and was a place for relaxation and casual visits from passers-by, especially in towns. Potted plants were commonly found on porches and even the meanest house would have some. Porches took many forms from white-columned galleries to simple stoops. Sometimes a porch would completely encircle a house and they often carried elaborate gingerbread trim on brackets, posts and railings.

Older houses sometimes had separate kitchens attached to the main house with a breezeway to protect the house from threat of fire from the cooking and to keep the heat out of the house. Rooms were heated in winter by fireplaces and wood or coal stoves. It was not unusual for every room in a house to have a fireplace or flue. In town, these fireplaces were adapted for the burning of coal; the firebox was not as wide and was very shallow and had a built-in coal grate. Wide hallways often went from the front of the house to the back and the high-ceilinged rooms opening to the center hall were cooled by breezes in summer. Before refrigeration, watermelons were often kept cool in the hall.

The "First Citizen of Buford" and his wife rock on their front porch, Sawnee Ave. and Wilson St., Buford, around the turn of the century. He was Bona Allen Sr. and she was Louisa Stanley. That house was moved in the 1930s to Sawnee Ave. near Shadburn Ferry Rd. The Allens built a 17-room mansion in 1912 on Main St. where they lived until their deaths. *(GWN 358-83)*

Reputed to be the oldest house in Suwanee, built in 1823, the Goodwin home has been in the family of Mrs. Mae Gilbert Burge for almost 150 years. It is located at 1471 Old Peachtree Road. Although a kitchen has been added and the home electrified, it is basically the same structure as in 1835 when William T. Graham sold it to his son-in-law, Joseph Goodwin, son of John Goodwin. *(Photo from Ben Baxter of Gwinnett Daily News)*

The James Albert Smith family *c.* 1914-15. Left to right: Lola, Louise, Daisy
(mother) holding Montine, Albert, Theo, Blondine and Hoke (on horse).
(Photo from Evelyn Green)

The Webb family gathers for a reunion in 1909 at the Andrew J. Webb house, built by James Flowers on Old Snellville Highway near Webb Gin House Road between Lawrenceville and Snellville. *Left to right* (on steps): Alton Langley, Ralph Cooper, Inez _____. Hazel Sawyer (m. H. B. Clower). *On porch*: neighbor child, Dr. Hiram Thomas Smith and wife Audrey Dixie Sawyer; Grover and Annie Sawyer; James Sawyer, co-founder of Snellville, and wife Emma Webb; Rev. Andrew Jackson Webb, long-time pastor of Friendship Primitive Baptist Church and wife Jane Braswell; Alex and Cora Webb; Jim and Daisy Webb with baby Golden Webb; Mae Langley with baby Taft, and Myrtice Cooper. On the balcony were uncles, aunts, and cousins. (*GWN 201*)

The William A. Minor family and dog in 1912 in front of their home, Rockbridge Road, south of U. S. 78 towards Centerville. *Left to right*: William A. Minor, Jr., W. A. Minor, Sr., Randall H. Minor, Ella Sue Minor, Mattie Wood Minor, Pauline Minor (m. James C. Pounds). Built in 1900, the house was remodeled in 1910 and again in 1970. (*GWN 75*)

Abe Russell, former slave, poses proudly before his Suwanee home, c. 1921.
(GWN 117)

Stop sign marking junction of Jackson Street with U.S. 29 was yellow with black lettering as were all stop signs in Georgia in the early 1950s when this photograph of the Reuben Smith house was taken. The superb Greek Revival structure with its Corinthian columns had another two decades to grace Lawrenceville before fire destroyed it about 1970. A Lawrenceville Post Office was later constructed on the site. (*GWN 288*)

The Bona Allen Mansion, a landmark during this century, is on the National Register of Historic Places. The 17-room Italian Renaissance Revival structure sits on a rise at the terminus of Main St., Buford. (*GHS Collection*)

The James Sawyer family in front of their home, North Road, Snellville c. 1901. Built by Sawyer, co-founder of Snellville, the "house of nine gables" was demolished in 1985. Posed here are, *left to right*: Grosvenor Mellville Sawyer, baby Hazel Editha Sawyer (m. H. B. Clower), James Sawyer, Frederick Charles Sawyer, Alice Emma (Webb) Sawyer, and Audrey Dixie Sawyer. (*GWN 194*)

Built in 1825 by Thomas Carroll, this home stood at the junction of U. S. 29, Rockbridge, and Harmony Grove roads until structural damage from termites caused it to be torn down in 1947. During Sherman's "March to the Sea," the Carrolls hid wheat between the walls where they had access to it from holes bored in the baseboards behind the master bed, the piano, and the sofa. There were four rooms below and two upstairs. Mrs. Mildred Martin, descendant of Carroll, erected a new house here in 1948, and preserved the huge tree, seen behind the well, after lightening killed it in 1975 at age 300. The well furnished water for many thirsty travelers between Lawrenceville and Atlanta. (*GWN 81*)

The James Robert Hood family, home, and 1914 Model T Ford on Alcovy Rd., Dacula. The house was built in 1910. *Left to right, front:* James Robert Hood, Lucille Hood (m. J. J. Moore), Mattie Loveless Hood, and (with bow tie) John J. Hood. *Rear:* Bobby Hood, Annie Hood (m. Paul Kelley) and Hugh L. Hood. (*GWN 265*)

49

Dr. Samuel Locklin Hinton, noted
physician and druggist, and his wife,
Alice Stanley, take an automobile
drive past their Dacula home before
1918. (*GWN 152*)

The building long known as the Sam J. Winn home on U. S. 29,
Lawrenceville, was built by Edward Steadman. J. P. Simmons bought it
from Steadman and gave it to his daughter Sarah when she married Sam
Winn in 1859. After Sarah Winn died in 1910, Mr. Winn sold the house
to O. A. Nix who remodeled it. Mr. and Mrs. L. M. Brand were the last
owners and after his death, Mrs. Brand continued to live there with her
children until July, 1940, when daughter Mamie and her bulldog
perished in the flames that consumed the house. (*Photo from Claude
Jordan*)

J. Mack Williams, his wife Della, and their children stand in front of their Snellville home in 1906. The children are, *left to right*: Essie (m. Wallace Mansfield), Broadus, Bernice (m. Guy Stephens) and Lillia (m. Claud E. Landrum). The house was demolished in 1976. (GWN 74)

George A. Burns homeplace in 1938 on what was then Norcross-Tucker Rd., now Jimmy Carter Blvd., Norcross. The house stood in northeast vicinity of what later became the intersection of Jimmy Carter Boulevard and I-85. During World War I, it was necessary for the family to leave home during the day because they were in the target area of the firing range located at today's intersection of Norcross-Tucker Road and Buford Highway. Lounging on the car were Sylvester Ross (left) and Clint Singleton. (*Photo from Delia Gilliland*)

54

The rich architectural gems that were homes to members of the Allen family in Buford are shown here. The sons of Bona Allen, Sr. built *opposite page, top,* the Bona Allen, Jr. house on Main Street, and *opposite lower,* the Wadleigh Allen house, known for many years as the Knight house and now destroyed, was on Sawnee Avenue; *above left* is the John Quincy Allen home now on the National Register, and *above right* the baronial home of Victor Allen on Sawnee Avenue. *(GHS Collection)*

Minor house, *c.* 1900, Annistown Rd., Centerville. The house was torn down in 1980. Note the decorative scrollwork across the roofline and above the gables. *(GWN 71)*

The William Albert Brogdon family gather in 1908 in front of their morning glory vine covered porch in Old Suwanee Baptist community, Sugar Hill district. *Left to right*: William Lester Brogdon with rifle, George Eldirge Brogdon, Tolbert Crayton Brogdon, Parilee (Dodd) Brogdon and husband Lounge Calhoun Brogdon, baby in carriage Abbie Sears (m. John Kelley), little girl Jessie Brogdon (m. Bonnie Mathis), behind carriage Hardy Terry (Jack) Brogdon, Mary Elizabeth (Martin) Brogdon and husband William Albert Brogdon, and daughter Mary Catherine Sears. (*GWN 143*)

58

The B. Ross Bolton family, 1907, outside their Beaver Ruin community home pose with their dog, "Dash" for a picture. *Left to right:* Virgil, Vic, Tillie, Grandma Cassie Martin, Ross and wife Elizabeth and Jessie Bee Bolton. The house on Bolton Circle underwent several additions. (*Photo from Tillie Bolton*)

The William Terrell home, built in 1823 on the former road from Hog Mountain to Lawrenceville, old U. S. 29, remained in the hands of descendants until it was destroyed by fire in 1987. In this 1895 photo, are, *left to right:* Charles Jenkins Terrell, Mack Spence Cornett, Kenan Troup Terrell Jr., Clara Rowland Terrell, Maria Maltbie Terrell and Mattie M. Dyer (child). The boy on the horse is Henry Terrell. (*GWN 344*)

Grass growing in yards was a sign of laziness in 1918 when Mattie Wages (m. James Fletcher Puckett) and her sister Alma Wages (m. Parks Phillips) swept their yard with brooms. The best brooms were made of dogwood branches. (*GWN 98*)

Among the oldest houses in Buford, this was built in 1867 by Adam Pool at the corner of Hill and Main Streets. It was moved in the 1930s to the corner of Hill and Moreno Streets. (*GWN 171*)

William E. Simmons, a lawyer and sometimes editor of the Lawrenceville News, built this, the last remaining house on the courthouse square in Lawrenceville about 1890. There he and his wife Mary Ambrose, became famous for entertaining Methodist ministers and for taking food to those in trouble.

Dr. W. P. Ezzard and his second wife, Doris Cooper, bought the house in the 1930s. There was once a windmill in the yard to bring water from the well, and the interior features English tiled fireplaces. The house was converted for office use while maintaining its character. (*Photo from Dick Corbin and Doug Eason*)

The N. G. Pharr family stand in front of their Dacula home in 1900. *Left to right*: Otis N. Pharr, Sallie Ewing Pharr, Newton Giles Pharr, Callie Pharr Wilson, Julian J. Wilson, Clara Pharr (m. Roscoe Sams), Etcel Pharr, Otho Jackson Pharr Sr., and the baby in front, Kathleen Wilson (m. Lewis Swann). (GWN 126)

The home of William Maltbie, Lawrenceville's first postmaster and long-time Gwinnett County Clerk of Inferior Court, on what became known as Maltbie Street. It was from this house that his wife Philadelphia Winn sallied forth to town to destroy a saloon whose barkeep was selling her son "the devil's brew" and ruining his life. The house was destroyed by fire in 1978. (*GWN 213*)

Anthony John L. Bates home on Old Peachtree Road and Cedar Drive near Lawrenceville was photographed in 1919. His grandson, Perrin Walker, age 7, sits on a horse while a friend waits his turn. Perrin's son, Jim Walker and wife, restored the old homestead. (*GWN 209*)

William Harrison Cooper and wife Elizabeth with five of their 13 children in front of their home, *c.* 1907, Highway 124, Braselton Road. Children l to r: Jimmac (baby in front), Estelle, Maybelle, DeeWitt Talmadge and Virginia Cooper. *(GWN 348)*

This Suwanee building, shown in 1912, has often been called the Rhodes Hotel. Daniel M. Born built a small house here and later gave it to his daughter Lillie when she married Henry W. Rhodes. They had seven children and added substantially to the house from time to time until it boasted six bedrooms and wide porches upstairs and down. Mr. Rhodes, a former school teacher, was head of the Suwanee School Board and enticed excellent teachers to Suwanee by allowing them to live in his home. After his death in 1911, Mrs. Rhodes took in more than one teacher at a time. *(Photo from Ann Lynn Link)*

"Flint Hill" on South Peachtree Street, Norcross, c. 1890. It was built by a Mr. Harris in 1835 who traded it and 800 surrounding acres to William McElroy in 1850 for a family of slaves. The front section seen here was added in 1870. In 1937 the house was remodeled to a Mount Vernon appearance by McElroy's granddaughter, Mrs. Harry Crider. Family ownership ended in 1978 when the house was sold outside the family. (GWN 44)

Fretwork and gingerbread decorate the Lankford home, also known as the
Tom and Temp Cooper home, on Rockbridge Road, Lilburn, c. 1900.
(*GWN 78*)

The Francis Ferdinand Juhan home in the 1880s faced the courthouse across Pike Street at Clayton Street in Lawrenceville. (*GWN 275*)

Mr. and Mrs. T. A. Clower stand in front of their Lenora Church Road home in Snellville in 1916. Saw-tooth sills distinguish the porch as do the knobs on the roofline. (GWN 202)

Opposite: William and Angie Hopkins Burns with their children, Arron and Olan Burns pose in front of their Lilburn home c. 1900. (*GWN 25*)

Homer Jones built this house at 218 Thrasher Street, Norcross. Later owners include Mr. and Mrs. L. D. Ewing who purchased it in 1930, and Mr. and Mrs. Steve Weathers. (*GWN 243*)

Children have always been popular with photographers and examples are seen here:

Lula Branch (m. House) and her doll as photographed in 1910.
(*GWN 39*)

Mrs. Effie Benson Pass and son Rudolph posed in 1909.
(*GWN 110*)

An unknown baby poses in 1900 in an ornate baby carriage recorded as owned by T. L. Roberts. The photographer was careless in allowing the backdrop to expose the bare ground. (*GWN 109*)

IN TOWN

The county seat, Lawrenceville, chartered December 15, 1821, was Gwinnett's first incorporated city. It was named for Capt. James Lawrence, a naval hero of the War of 1812, who proclaimed after being mortally wounded, "Don't give up the ship." The four streets forming the courthouse square, Crogan, Pike, Perry and Clayton, were named for highly respected men: George Croghan and Commodore Perry, heroes of the War of 1812; Zebulon M. Pike, soldier and explorer; and Augustin Smith Clayton, judge and congressman.

The communities of Hog Mountain in the east and Pinckneyville in the west predate the county by several years although neither was incorporated. Other communities sprang up here and there; the most viable, Gloster, Centerville, Luxomni, continue their existence while less fortunate ones disappeared after a time. One settlement that actually did disappear was Bettstown near the Apalachee River in an area that is now in Barrow County. It sank into the ground and the last seen of it in 1903 was the gables and roofs protruding from the moist earth.

The Georgia Air Line Railroad had been chartered under leadership of Jonathan Norcross just before the War Between the States intervened in its construction. The rail line was reorganized in 1869 as the Atlanta Charlotte Air Line, and during that year the line had been constructed as far as Howell's Crossroads, today's Duluth. On October 26, 1870, Norcross became the county's second chartered city, fifty nine years after the first. The railroad was completed through Gwinnett County in 1871, the year of the founding of Gwinnett's third and fourth cities, Buford and Duluth. Suwanee, while contemporary with Buford, Norcross and Duluth, was not officially chartered until many years later. Falling on hard times and receiving name changes, the Atlanta Charlotte Air Line became a part of the Southern Railroad on July 18, 1894, and the line has prospered since.

The Georgia, Carolina and Northern Railroad, soon to become the Seaboard Air Line Railroad, was completed in 1892 and the first passenger train entered Atlanta

Rawlins Store, Main Street, Snellville, opened in 1917 and closed in 1952. This 1935 photograph shows James Carl Ford, Leonard Brownlee, Emmett O. Clower, William L. Knight, Jim Rawlins, and proprietor Walter L. Rawlins. The chair at rear of store behind the wood heater became a barber chair on Saturdays when Jim Rawlins left his farm chores to cut hair for the public. Hooks on the ceiling held bananas and dry goods were sold in other parts of the store located west of intersection of U. S. 78 and SR 124. (*Photo from Kathryn Bird*)

on Sunday April 24, 1892. This railroad brought into being the towns of Auburn, Dacula and Lilburn.

Grayson was called Trip when it was founded in 1871, Lilburn was once known as Bryan, Braden or McDaniel, and Snellville was once New London. Sugar Hill, Rest Haven and Berkeley Lake are other cities within the county. Loganville, since its chartering in 1887, has always sat on the Gwinnett-Walton county line.

Lawrenceville, looking west on Crogan Street, innocent of paving in 1912. Stores at center left face courthouse square, which was fenced. Tall building at end was the three-story Cornett Hotel, later Button Gwinnett Hotel. *(GWN 1927)*

Norcross on a busy day *c.* 1900, trading cotton on South Peachtree between Jones St. and Holcomb Bridge Rd. Cotton was shipped from Norcross to Savannah, thence to England. Merchants seen in this photo include R. A. Gant, A. A. Johnson, T. Edwin Johnson and ———— Kinnett. *(GWN 255)*

Cotton trading on Main St., Buford in mid-1920s. Many of the buildings still stand. Buford was chartered 1871 with W. B. Haygood as first mayor. *(GWN 93)*

Some of these buildings pictured here in 1925 on Perry St., facing the courthouse in Lawrenceville predate the War Between the States and the saloon torn up by Philadelphia Maltbie was located on this block. The Strand Theatre, center, was owned by E. T. Hopkins who charged only 10 cents admission. Above the movie house was the Oddfellows Hall. *(GWN 214)*

Facing page: Main Street in Dacula in 1905. The buildings at right abutted the Seaboard Railroad and were used in shipping cotton and other commodities. This area was first known as Chinquapin Grove when it moved to the work camp set up by the railroad in 1891. The name was changed to Hoke to honor a railroad official, but the railroad refused to allow the train to stop at a place with such a name. So John Freeman mixed some letters from the names of Atlanta and Decatur and came up with Dacula, which was approved. The city was incorporated in 1905 with Dr. Samuel L. Hinton as first mayor. *(GWN 124)*

Downtown Grayson looked like this in 1947. Buildings at left are gone now, and those at right no longer have tin-roofed awnings over the sidewalk. Jacobs General Store, across State Road 20 in center of photograph closed after many years of business and the building later housed other businesses. (*Photo from Herman Fowler*)

The Brunswick Hotel at Thrasher and Jones street, Norcross, in 1910, was built in 1870 by John Thrasher with 29 rooms and a dining room which catered to local people. It went out of business in 1930, due to the Depression and was rented out as apartments until demolished in 1951 to build a Post Office at that spot. (GWN 272)

James Sawyer, seated, and his brother-in-law, William Langley, were proprietor and clerk of Sawyer's General Merchandise Store in Snellville and were photographed in 1890. This rock store with its arched windows and cupola was located at intersection of U. S. 78 and State Road 124 and was demolished in early 1970s to make room for a gas station. (*GWN 197*)

The stagecoach used to stop at Choice's Store and Post Office. From 1830-34 Jacob Crow, riding a horse, picked up and delivered mail here enroute from Lawrenceville to Fayetteville. The building, with later additions, stood for about 100 years at what later became   U. S. 29 and Rockbridge Road, Lilburn. Its first postmaster, Tulley Choice of DeKalb County, appointed in 1824, was followed by John Choice, William McDaniel, William Crowell, George B. Hudson, Thomas Carroll and Thomas Matthews. For many years before it was torn down in 1930, it was known as Carroll's Store. It was a cotton buying and mercantile center, and in the 1920s, milliners used to come from Atlanta to trim hats in the dry goods section. Much of the land surrounding it has been developed commercially. (*Photo from Mildred Carroll Martin*)

Roy E. Johnson lounges in front of John B. Brogdon's General Store in Suwanee c. 1920. (*GWN 122*)

This whimsical shot was posed in 1915 as a protest against puddles in front of businesses in downtown Lawrenceville. Charles Mason and son, Clarence, at right, led the protest by shooting at supposed fish in the puddle. Two gentlemen on left seine the puddle while others fish with canes. The boy at right center has just caught an enormous fish and the watermelons at his feet may have been used for bait. (*GWN 12*)

These buildings in this 1900 photograph of downtown Duluth faced both Peachtree Street and the railroad. Duluth was originally called Howell's Cross Roads and a depot was built here in 1871. Evan Howell was invited to make a speech and name the town at the depot dedication and the name he chose was the same as an obscure town in Minnesota receiving publicity at the time: Duluth. (*GWN 262*)

Snellville men gather in front of Albert Pate's store in 1910, Scenic Highway north of U.S. 78. The building was torn down in the 1970s. Mr. Pate is the one in white shirt with bow tie. (*GWN 29*)

Workers pose inside Haynes' Grocery in
Buford in the 1920s. *(GWN 135)*

Salesladies Mrs. Liller Cain, Mrs. Bell Cole and Mrs. Sylvester Cain await
customers in Cain's Dry Goods Store in Norcross in early 1900s. Popular items
for sale were Vanida hair nets and Sure Thing nest eggs, china eggs left in hen
nests to encourage the laying of eggs. Sometimes people had to make do with
porcelain door knobs that fooled the hens just as well. The store was built by
R. O. Medlock late 1890s. *(GWN 256)*

Albert Dyer, behind counter with bow tie, ran a store from 1887 to 1891 for Maria Terrell and Mack Spence Cornett. The man at right examines a bolt of checkered cloth. The store was located in Lawrenceville near the Cornett Hotel. (*GWN 341*)

Payne Brothers & Huff Hardware store of 1920s in Duluth faced the railroad on lower floor and Peachtree Street on the upper floor. *Left to right*: Lee Payne, Jesse Payne, and Tom Huff. (*Photo from Minor Corley*)

Long-time Norcross businesses include Burnett's Store, at
the corner of Peachtree and Cemetery Streets, which served
the people of Norcross for 100 years. (*GWN 77*)

Lounging in front of W. M. Keady Drug Store, Norcross,
about 1911, *left to right:* B. C. Cain, L. Herb Letson and
Henry Lively. (GWN 254)

Interior of Lawrenceville's first electric light plant on Mechanic, now Jackson, Street was caught by a photographer on April 18, 1906. *(GWN 229)*

A parade launches Clean-Up Week in Buford in the 1950s and passes an ill-omened section of town; no institution pictured here has survived. The Bona Allen saddlery has closed; long gone is L. A. Wilson Furniture and Piano Co. The Buford Commercial Bank became a part of NBG and lost its identity, and another identity was lost at the bank when the building's fine facades facing Main and Harris streets were stripped of moldings and woodwork and disguised behind stucco and smoked glass. The four buildings at right were destroyed by two separate fires in mid 1950s: first to go were Doc Simpson's Grocery Store and Prickett's 5-10-25¢ Store, followed sometime later by Ramey's Ready-to-Wear and Leak's Grocery. Ironically, these stores replaced a hotel and other stores burned in the early years of the century. *(Photo from Billy Cain)*

ON THE MOVE

Horses and mules were the method of transportation during the county's first century. The animals were adaptable; the same animal that plowed and operated farm equipment would pull the family to town on Saturday, and to church on Sunday. The advent of the automobile in the first years of this century revolutionized our way of living and doing things. People were no longer limited to working within miles of their homes. As automobiles became more numerous, better roads became necessary. U. S. Highway 29 was paved in 1929, becoming the county's first paved highway. In 1943 there were less than 97 miles of paved roads within the county. Twenty years later, Interstate 85 was under construction and was completed in 1965.

With the use of automobiles came the need for fuels and products for the car. Enterprising businessmen installed gas pumps in front of their stores and began catering to the automobile people long before service stations came to the county. The first gas pumps were hand operated; a crank was turned by hand, pumping the gasoline into the glass reservoir at the top of the pump. Scales inside the reservoir were marked in increments of gallons, and when the customer pumped up the amount he needed, he put the hose into the fuel tank of the automobile, tripped a lever, and the fuel flowed by gravity into the vehicle.

The railroad that became the Southern came through the county in 1871 and the Seaboard came in 1892. A narrow gauge railroad connected Lawrenceville to the Southern line at Suwanee in 1881. Yet another railroad was completed in 1898, also narrow gauge, connecting the Seaboard line at Lawrenceville with Grayson and Loganville. Lawrenceville at the turn of the century had thus become the hub of a network of rail lines connecting it with Suwanee, Grayson, Loganville, and the Seaboard and Southern rail systems.

Salesman at wheel, drives *left to right:* Dr. Virgil G. Hopkins, Ezekiel T. Hopkins and wives, Mrs. Eula (Lowe) Hopkins and Mrs. Mae (Rogers) Hopkins, in new 1912 Buick. The Hopkins brothers had the first Buick and Ford agency in Gwinnett County. *(GWN 261)*

In 1919, Vance Motor Co., facing Main Street, Buford, sold Overland automobiles. In its basement was Gunter's Garage and repair shop with entrance from Jones Alley. Dewitt Gunter, right, and Jess Wheeler, second from left, and other mechanics were among those who helped keep Gwinnett people on the move. Behind them is a Model-T with a modern development of that day - a spare tire on the rear. (*Photo from Wendell Fuller*)

Horses, mules, wagons, and buggies fill the parking lot in Buford on Saturday, October 24, 1908. Stables at left are at corner of Garnett Street and Jones Alley at site of Old City Hall. House at extreme right sits at corner of Moreno and Garnett Streets. (*Photo from Billy Cain*)

John M. Barnett and W. Jack Stancil stand in front of their wagon and buggy shop on North Road, Snellville, on a winter day in 1900. Through the barren trees at left can be seen the Sawyer House.
(*GWN 30*)

Opposite: Patterson's Blacksmith Shop, *far right*, sat at the corner of Culver and Pike Streets in this 1900 Lawrenceville photograph. The building on left housed a woodworking shop on the ground floor and wagons were built on the second floor. Pictured, left to right, A. T. Patterson, Stone Bush, Weymon Cooper, John Herrington, Jim Patterson, Tandy Patterson, Richard Bush, Scott Davis, Tandy Herrington shoeing a horse, A. T. Patterson, Sr., Nell Bagwell, and Lois Patterson (m. Paris). The horse named "Tobe" was owned by Charlie Cooper, postman, who used him on the mail route. (*Photo from Sara McCutchen*)

THIS IS THE BOY THAT LAID
THE BOLT THAT THREW 38

Opposite: Clouds of steam billow as spectators take in train wreck on Southern Railroad just above West's Crossing in 1908. This is present location of State Road 20 bridge over Southern Railroad at former Mangum's Crossing in Sugar Hill. (*GWN 177*)

The inscription on this 1908 photograph reads, "This is the boy that laid the bolt that threw 38." Twelve year old Louis Cooksey was accused of placing a bolt on the tracks, causing the wreck of Southern train # 38 south of Buford on Sunday, May 23, 1908. This wreck brought about the deaths of the engineer, B. F. Dewberry, and fireman, Mayson Wadkins. Cooksey was tried and found innocent of these charges. (*GWN 186*)

The rails brought into being most of Gwinnett's towns and each of those had its own depot. Trains no longer stop at the Norcross depot, above, where Tom Rochester, depot agent, stands at the door. The depot, sold to the town by the Southern Railroad, has been adapted for other uses and is maintained in a manner that adds much to the atmosphere of the downtown area. (*GWN 258*)

Signs over the doors of the Suwanee depot, *right*, indicated "separate but equal" accommodations for "White" and "Colored" passengers, as did all the facilities of the time. This building and adjacent sheds and warehouses also served the narrow gauge railroad linking Suwanee and Lawrenceville up to the early 1920s. (*GWN 120*)

Workmen scrape and repair Perry Street in Lawrenceville in the 1920s. Robert Henry Wade sits on tractor at left. (*GWN 331*)

Lawrenceville-Suwanee Railroad Station in Lawrenceville at the time the narrow gauge rails were being converted to standard gauge. After the line closed, the station became Sammon Lumber Company. When the building was destroyed by fire it had long been Cooper's Feed Store. Among those pictured here: Ed Shackelford, section crew foreman; Charlie McKelvey; Ed McKelvey; Bob McKelvey; and Truman Brogdon. (*Photo from Mrs. Jack Brogdon*)

The horse and buggy were primary means of
transportation in 1910-15 when S. J. Puckett
and his dog posed near Buford. (GWN 164)

A period of transition can be seen in this 1910 photograph. James A. Daniel drives the new Buick of Jesse Smith, seated in what today would be the driver's seat. Passengers in back seat are Allen C. Daniel, at left, and Mr. Massey. The building in the background, Mr. Daniel's blacksmith shop which would soon fall into disuse, was on the Daniel farm on Old Norcross Road near Lawrenceville. (*GWN 224*)

In 1926, 4H girls from Gravel Springs and Hopewell display canning they have prepared to enter in the Gwinnett Agricultural and Industrial Fair. Placards on Pharr's store advertise Coca Cola, Star Brand tobacco and the county fair. The fair signs are left over from a previous year with the dates altered. From *left to right:* Dana Funderburk (m. ——— Roper), Ruth Braswell, Nellie Pharr, Carrie Fuller (m. Guy Russell), Elizabeth Sudderth, Eula Mae Fuller (m. Eural Holland) and Flora Nell Funderburk. The car belonged to their home demonstration agent, Lena Bess Medlock. *(GWN 46 & 189)*

At right: The Texaco Star proclaims sale of that brand gasoline at the Brogdon Store, Railroad Avenue, Sugar Hill. Also for sale at the store were dry goods, groceries, notions, and sundries. *(GWN 181)*

IN CHURCH

The settlement of Gwinnett County was part of the western migration and expansion of the United States. Many pioneers of Gwinnett originally came from the piedmont of Virginia and the Carolinas. The next generation found some of them in Louisiana or Texas by way of Alabama. These folks generally were of Scottish, English, and Welsh extraction, and most were Methodist, Baptist, or Presbyterian.

Closely following the establishment of homesteads and farms were church buildings. Mount Moriah Baptist in Duncan's district near the Barrow County line is believed to be the oldest in the county. Early records, if kept, have been lost, but the cornerstone of the church proclaims 1779 as the date of its organization. Family and church traditions bear out this early date, give or take a few years, and the fact that this headright section was a part of Franklin County as early as 1784 adds more credence to the claim. Zoar Methodist at Centerville has a history almost as old, having been organized in 1811, and like Mount Moriah, its early records have been lost. The organizing of churches have appeared to occur in spurts; the 1820s saw the births of a number of well known churches as did the 1850s and the 1880s.

In earlier years churches often had services only once a month, allowing families to attend four different churches during the month; one minister might serve several churches at one time. This brought the phenomenon of one family with children having their church membership at various churches.

Revivals were held in the summer, usually at laying-by time, when farm families could indulge themselves with both day and evening meetings. Baptizings followed the "meeting week" and new converts and those rededicating their lives were taken into the "liquid grave" usually a lake or pond, and immersed individually under the water. After changing clothes, those baptized stood in a receiving line inside the church near the front, and the congregation marched by, offering them the "right hand of church fellowship."

Death is not vanishing but many of the customs dealing with death are disappearing. In the past, neighbors and close family did the washing and dressing

The Fairview Presbyterian Church, organized August 9, 1823, is seen in this 1909 photograph. This building was erected by James S. Russell on what became State Route 120 near its intersection with Highway 316 in Lawrenceville. The steeple, and entryway were since altered, and additions were built in the rear. (*GWN 59*)

of the deceased and the corpse did not leave home until the funeral hour. Clocks were stopped and photographs and mirrors were covered or turned to the wall. Family, friends, and neighbors brought food to the home of the deceased and many remained overnight in what was called a "sitting up" where all-night vigils were kept. Burials were usually done the next day in the times before embalming; in the summer the burial was done immediately with the funeral service following the next Sunday. The funeral might include three or more preachers and each might speak for an hour, continuing until family and friends were reduced to grief-stricken tears. The high point of the funeral was when the congregation, followed by close friends, then family members, marched by the open coffin and looked upon the deceased for the last time. The immediate family, witnessing the public grief of their relatives and friends became more emotional when their turn came, precipitating more demonstrations and faintings.

Lawrenceville Presbyterian Church about 1912, on Oak Street. Erected in 1830s as a branch of Fairview until 1891, when it organized a separate church. Sold to Primitive Baptists, later abandoned. Inset: Rev. Jos. Marcus Harris, pastor 1910. *(Photo from Mary Alice Juhan)*

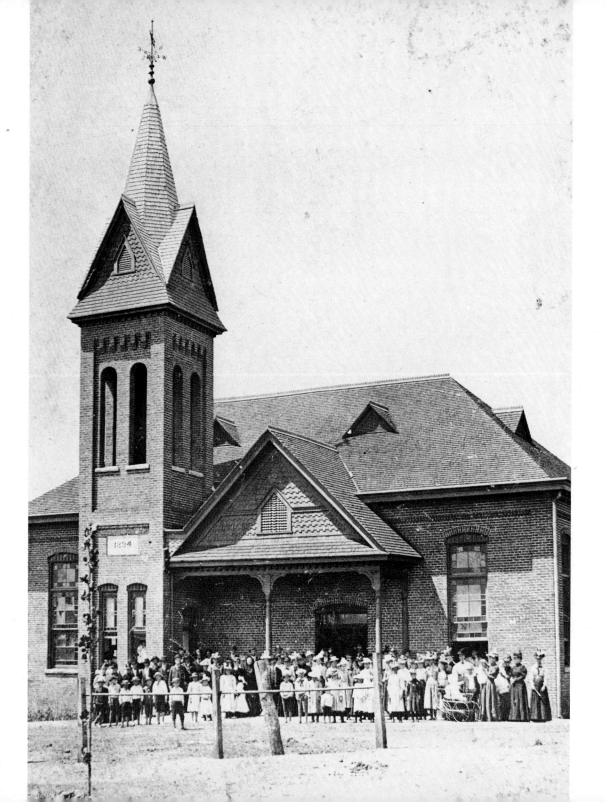

Left: The congregation of the First Methodist Church of Buford stand in front of their building on Scott Street in the early 1900s. This was their home from 1894 until they moved to a new facility at corner of Main and Hill Streets in 1926. This building, sans steeple and porch, subsequently became a funeral home, an Oldsmobile dealership, an automobile garage, and a warehouse for antique auto parts. (*GWN 170*)

Norcross (First) Baptist Church was founded 17 May, 1872, and Rev. William Mooney Davis was its first pastor. Meetings were first held at the Community House, alternating with the Methodists and the Presbyterians until each congregation could build its own house of worship. The Baptists later built this building on the northwest corner of Peachtree and Jones Streets. In the 1960s, First Baptist built a new structure on Old Peachtree Road and the Galilean Baptist Church met here until moving to Holcomb Bridge Road. The historic facility then became home to Episcopalians as Christ Church. (*GWN 251*)

Gwinnett Place Mall and other development on Pleasant Hill Road northeast of I-85 cover the area used in this 1925 baptizing for Pleasant Hill Baptist Church. It was then Charlie Lester's pasture. Preacher W. M. Williams, right, baptizes Virgil O'Shields. Sixty-four were immersed that day requiring assistance from Preacher Marshall Still. Others to be baptized were: Polly Guthrie (m. George Brannon), Exie Franklin, Clarence Williams, Corrine O'Shields, Aubrey Franklin, Vera Williams (m. Floyd O'Kelly), Mary Reese, Bertie Montgomery, Mrs. Lathem, Priscilla Lathem, Ozzie Franklin, George Corley, Bonnie Mauldin, Esto Corley, Chloe Shackelford (m. John Montgomery). *Also*: Howard Cruse, Lola Mae Bailey, Alice Murrell, Early Mauldin, Addie Zoo Garmon, Jessie Bee Cain, Lynn Cain, Lucille Davis, and Angie Franklin. *Others in photograph*: Lena Wells Williams, Lois Wells, Mary Franklin, Lettie Givens, Lucille Mauldin, Pauline Wells, Georgia O'Kelly, Lloyd O'Kelly, Wynell O'Kelly, Lara Franklin, Annie Maude Adams, Nora Adams, Preacher Still, Madge Franklin, Fannie Franklin, Thomas Franklin, Emma Wright, Murel Davis, Pearl Davis, Mollie Givens, and Lois McCurley. (*Photo from Hoyt Tuggle*)

Baptismal service of Hebron Baptist Church c. 1916 at James Wilson's fish pond, Dacula. Rev. J. A. Crumbley is about to baptize Blanche Wood. Waiting for baptism, *left to right*: Jewel Nash, Annie Mae Etheridge, Bert Maughon, Ada Sikes, and Elmina Etheridge. Observers are, *back row third from right*: John Barnard, fourth, Hoyt Hamilton; sixth, R. P. Hood. *At left on back row*, Oscar Smith. At edge of water, *left*: Jim Wilson, and on banks at left: J. G. Hood; third, Ruth Hood; fifth, Mrs. Oscar Smith; next two were singers from Atlanta. (*Photo from John Hood*)

The first sermon in the Lawrenceville Methodist Church was held in a temporary log courthouse before 1823. Their first church was on the corner of Pike and Crogan Streets. When that building burned, the congregation moved in 1845 to a new one on the hill on Oak Street. The building in this photograph is the third church building of the Methodists and was built in 1891 with a weathervane on the shingled steeple and a window featuring the Star of David. In 1902, a fire originating here destroyed this church and the Lawrenceville Public School next door. (*GWN 249*)

The steep-roofed building seen behind the silent city of the dead was home to Duncan Creek Congregational Church for seventy-one years. Shortly after its founding in 1855, a log church was built but was replaced by this house of worship in 1889. This structure on SR 124 near Buford was torn down in 1960 to make way for a brick building. (*GWN 94*)

Members of Old Suwanee Baptist Church celebrate with dinner on the grounds in 1908. These festivities are still carried out in rural areas and are sometimes referred to as all-day-to-do, or homecoming day. *(GWN 113)*

Participants leave Harmony Grove Methodist
Church, near Auburn, at the conclusion of an
all-day singing, akin to all-day-to-do. Harmony
Grove was in Gwinnett County in 1908 when this
photograph was taken but has been in Barrow
County since 1914. *(GWN 267)*

Week-long revivals or camp meetings are held in this arbor at Lawrenceville Methodist camp grounds located on 50 acres on Braselton Road. In 1832, five men each donated $10.00 to purchase the land. Families camped there, sang, prayed, ate and visisted for a week in summer after crops were laid by. *(GWN 237)*

This building of the (First) Baptist Church of Snellville was constructed in 1883 shortly after the organizing of the church on August 12, 1882, and was replaced in 1946. Picture dates from late 1880s. *(GWN 198)*

The Methodist Church in Norcross as it appeared in the 1900s. This church, originally called Flint Hill Methodist, was established in the 1820s about one mile from what became Norcross. The congregation moved to Norcross about the time of the city's chartering in 1871 and this house of worship was built in 1875. When the Methodists built their new church in 1968, this building became home to the congregation of St. Patrick Roman Catholic Church. When the Catholics built a new home on Beaver Ruin Road in 1981, this facility became home to other denominations. (*GWN 248*)

The Lawrenceville First Baptist Church as seen in 1951 before construction of new sanctuary. Services were first held in this building on October 14, 1900. This church was organized on May 2, 1840, when a number of members from Redlands Baptist Church left to found a new church. Steeples, brickwork and stained glass have been removed or altered to conform with contemporary architecture of later additions. (*Photo from GHS Collection*)

This old steel bell stands silently among the dead in the Haynes Creek Primitive Baptist Church cemetery, a reminder of days long ago when its clear ringing chimes summoned farmers to bring picks and shovels to the cemetery to dig a grave for a neighbor. The cemetery is on Rosebud Road, South of U. S. 78. The bell used to be mounted on a scaffold at tree top level so its ringing could be heard for miles. *(Photo from Roy E. Hutchens Collection)*

Prospect Methodist Church was organized in 1830 and this twin-steepled building was built in 1880. It was expanded and altered in the intervening years before a new sanctuary was added in 1988. (*GWN 289*)

The Lawrenceville Methodist Church was rebuilt on Pike Street following the 1902 fire which destroyed both the Lawrenceville school and the church in its former location on Oak Street. This 1923 photograph shows the fourth building of the Methodists with its Corinthian capitals, later removed, still on their pilasters. When the Methodists moved in 1970s, this facility became home to other church denominations.
(*GWN 240*)

Drambliss Whitlock, on right with hat, and his Singing School Class at Alcovy Baptist Church in 1915. Shaped notes were taught at these singing schools and each shape had its name: do, re, mi, fa, sol, la, and ti. Sometimes fa-sol-la singings were held at churches where the names of the notes were sung instead of the words. Alcovy Church was organized in 1828 and prospered until the time of the War Between the States when it went into decline. It was reorganized in 1868 and has been active since that time.
(*GWN 316*)

135

AT WORK

Those who worked anywhere but on the farm were considered employed at "public work." This included any regular job away from home. Before the automobile, a man could work at blacksmith shops, sawmills, and in town. In the waning years of the last century and the opening years of this century, many were forced to move to Atlanta and other cities to obtain adequate work. Many left the countryside after World War II for the town in order to carpool to Atlanta and Doraville where jobs were offered.

Before the War Between the States, a Southerner's idea of a factory was that of a cotton mill. Lawrenceville Manufacturing Company, founded in 1851, later manufactured goods for the Confederates until it burned in 1864. A second cotton mill was established around 1900 and continued in operation until the 1930s. That building was taken over by General Shoe Company and operated until the early 1970s.

No company left its mark so deeply and for so long a time as did the Bona Allen Company, founded in 1873 in Buford. The business grew rapidly, requiring more and more employees, and many farmers moved to Buford to work there. It eventually included an oil mill extracting oil from cotton seed, and factories producing horse collars, saddles, shoes, glue, and the original harness factory and tannery.

People flocked to the "depression proof" town looking for work. Even in the worst of times, the country's farmers had to replace worn out leather goods, available from the Allen company. At its height, more than 2,000 people were employed there.

In Norcross, Edward F. Buchanan, on orphan born in 1871, hung around the Norcross depot learning telegraphy from the agent there. At age 13 he went west and later returned with royalties from his inventions, and established United Electrical Manufacturing Co. which and assembled several automobiles called the Nor-X.

The GENESCO factory, Lawrenceville, seen from the air in 1950. GENESCO stood for General Shoe Company. The tower was on the corner of the original building built in 1900 for the Lawrenceville Cotton Mill, and the subsequent additions to the structure can be seen as well as fields under cultivation beyond the Seaboard Railroad. When this building on Buford Drive near the Seaboard Railroad was demolished in the 1970s, the timbers of yellow pine were saved and sold for reuse.
(*GWN 293*)

The interior of the Lawrenceville Cotton Mills can be seen in this 1920s photograph. *(GWN 241)*

At right: Plesy Jones operates his steam sorghum mill near Yellow River in 1912. This was one of the first syrup mills operated by steam. Mr. Jones, with beard and hat, stands between the boiler where the steam was made and the evaporator where the steam cooked the juices from the canes into syrup. *(GWN 112)*

Todd's Brickyard, October 1910, where the employees worked six 10-hour days and earned one dollar per day. This facility was located near Lilburn. *(GWN 36)*

Workmen reroof the Alcovy School with wooden shingles in early 1920s. *(Photo from Horace McAdams)*

The grist mill was a most important operation to the farmer where his dried corn would be ground into corn meal. The best meal was ground in water powered mills as the grinding was slow. Later, mills operated by steam or electricity, ground so fast it "cooked" the meal.

Opposite: What is now known as Freeman's Mill was built on the Alcovy River in 1866 by John and Levi Loveless using mortise and tenon joints joined by pegs. Later it was operated by Jacksons, Freemans, Pharrs, and Swanns. (*GWN 232*)

Above right: Henry Johnson Puckett and Alvin Givens have left their corn and await its grinding in 1912 at Freeman's Mill. (*GWN 92*)

Below right: The rusting wheel and dam across Ivy Creek were all that remained of Woodward's Mill after a fire in 1978. Shadrack Bogan built this mill in 1824 on a site that later would be adjacent to the intersection of State Road 20 and I-85 near Buford. Other families associated with the mill in its 150 year history were: Woodward, Davis, and Pharr. (*GHS Collection*)

143

Jim Dempsey, *at left*, waits for his corn to be ground at Hopkins Mill in 1950. The mill was located off Beaver Ruin Road near I-85 and was destroyed by fire. It left its name in the form of Hopkins Mill subdivision and Pond Road and Old Hopkins Mill Road. (*GWN 54*)

Sims Brothers' rig pulls a huge log in the Bethesda Community, 1915, the likes of which will not be seen in the county for many years. (*GWN 302*)

Bill Tribble owned this roving sawmill. The boiler at left operated the saw in center by means of wide belt. Pictured here are Griff Lord at the engine; Hamp Tribble in two-mule wagon; owner, Bill Tribble in vested suit; log turner is one of Langley boys who lived on J. O. Whitworth place nearby. Frank Booth operates the lever of the saw. Driving the log cart pulled by two spotted oxen is Wade Davis who entertained others with his yodeling. Photo made behind farms of Lindsey Watson and Berry Smith on New Hope Road outside of Lawrenceville. *(Cleo Booth Ritchie Collection)*

146

Workers using Frank Booth's sawmill below Tribble Mill prepare to convert to boards the heart pine forest on the Mary Tribble estate. *Left to right:* Griff Lord and Carl Davis at the steam engine. Charlie Townley operates the saw and Frank and Edgar Booth feed the logs. Less Langley drives the log cart pulled by oxen, Alex and Oscar. *(Cleo Booth Ritchie Collection)*

Robert H. Allen, founder of Harness Shop in 1867 in what became Buford, sits in his goat cart surrounded by employees. Because "Mr. R. H." was lame, he traveled in a goat cart. *(GWN 137)*

The 1981 fire that destroyed Bona Allen Tannery was not its first. In this 1903 photograph, tannery employees clean up still-smoking rubble. Barrel vats *at left* were replaced by steel ones when tannery was rebuilt. In the foreground, hides which survived the fire hang up to dry. *(Photo from Robert F. Saine)*

Tannery Street, left foreground, was paved with cobblestones shortly after this picture was taken in May 1897. This street led by the wooden tannery buildings destroyed by fire in 1903 to an earlier home of Bona Allen, Sr., at extreme left, the only building still standing in 1984. (*GWN 355-83*)

Nothing in this 1940 photograph of the Bona Allen Tannery remains. The great fire of December, 1981, consumed all buildings except the smokestack which was felled a few days later. Highly prized are the glazed white brick laid in the courses of red brick in the smokestack that proudly proclaimed BONA ALLEN, INC. (*GWN 354-83*)

Men and young boys take a break at the shingle
mill about 1910 near depot, Lawrenceville. *(GWN
343)*

Workers and families at peach cannery in Sugar Hill *c.*
1899. Machines on table peel the fruit. Woman in center
holding jar of peaches is Mary Dodd. *(GWN 187)*

Summerour Cotton Gin, Norcross, c. 1930. Farmers wait their turns in trucks or atop their crop of cotton. (*Photo from Dave Magoon*)

Arthur Johnson and J. W. Darby weigh a cotton bale at a Centerville gin and warehouse in 1935. (*GWN 205*)

AT SCHOOL

The first known school in the county was the Lawrenceville Academy. In 1822 the Inferior Court issued an order that ten acres on the hill northwest of town be laid off and reserved for schools. An 1832 deed to the Trustees of Lawrenceville Academy included ten acres in town lot 79 and carried the clause that churches might also be built on the property with the approval of the school trustees. Gwinnett Manual Labor Institute in Lawrenceville established by 1834 was run by ministers of Fairview Presbyterian Church.

Boys were sent to school, if possible, but girls were not educated other than at home. Therefore, the Lawrenceville Female Seminary was founded to remedy this situation. Incorporated in 1837 by an act of the General Assembly in Milledgeville, the first building for the seminary was built at the present corner of South Perry and Seminary streets. This building burned in 1850 or 51 and was replaced c. 1855 with a two-story Federal style brick structure that was completely restored in the 1970s. Privately, George Hopkins of Pinckneyville contracted in 1830 to teach 25 students at $8.00 a year in William Wardlaw's house.

Free public-supported schools began in 1870. Schools, mostly one-room buildings were at or near a church. Many took the name of the church; others the community name. At least two churches took the name of the earlier school: Gravel Springs and Ivy Creek. During the depression of 1930s, Bethesda School was built by unemployed men of the community. The city school system in Buford was established before 1884 and in Lawrenceville in 1893, and city schools were established in Grayson and Norcross, and perhaps other cities. Consolidation of the county schools was effected in the 1950s when all schools in the county with the exception of the Buford system which remained independent, merged into the Gwinnett County school system with six high schools: Central Gwinnett in Lawrenceville; West Gwinnett in Norcross; South Gwinnett in Snellville; North Gwinnett in Suwanee; Dacula in Dacula; and Hooper-Renwick in Lawrenceville for black students. West was later renamed Norcross and Duluth was revived.

In this century, communities were proud of their schools and much energy went into the design of the larger schools. Some were eclectic with elaborate architecture and others were more subdued. Most had cupolas or steeples with bells that were rung at opening and closing of the school day. Blackboards were made of real slate

The Lawrenceville Female Seminary building, corner South Perry and Seminary streets, was built c. 1855 to replace the original 1837 structure destroyed by fire. On National Register of Historic Places. (GWN 233)

and were really black. Children carried their lunches in pails. Even into this century the school year was geared to the farmers' schedule with no sessions during critical planting and harvesting times so the children might participate in the necessary chores at home. Before the 1930s children were expected to walk to school, becoming part of the legend of walking miles through the ice and snow to get an education.

The Norcross High School in 1945. *(GWN 253)*

The Lawrenceville City School in 1900 had less than two years left before it would be destroyed by fire. This building was built on Oak Street in 1895 and was the first tax-funded public school in that town. (*GWN 250*)

Opposite: The second city school in Lawrenceville was opened in 1903, although the sign in the arch on the second floor says 1902. This building was occupied until 1923 when it was torn down in favor of a larger building which was later burned by an arsonist. A replacement building built on the same site in 1948 served as a school and later as Gwinnett County Administration Building until completion of the Gwinnett Justice and Administration Center. (*GWN 266*)

MASONIC HALL
BUFORD GA.

187-5

The first brick school in Buford, long known as the Old Academy, was built in 1884. It became home to the Masons as indicated in this 1923 photograph when the building had fallen on hard times. The Spring Street landmark fell victim to fire in 1987 when it was totally destroyed. (*GWN 144*)

The nucleus of the Old School on Church Street, Buford, was dedicated in 1906. The school was later expanded in the rear to Jackson Street, the high school, at right, was added, and the auditorium, never completed, was added at left. The High School was moved to Hill Street in 1949 and the Elementary School followed in the spring of 1956. After the other buildings were abandoned, the auditorium functioned for years as gymnasium for the Colored School and was standing while other buildings had burned or been torn down. (*Photo from Billy Cain*)

Above: The Snellville High School was built of Snellville granite in 1927 on what became U.S. 78 East. When the building was demolished in the late 1970s, granite blocks were saved and used to build rock walls and paving for public areas of the Lanier Water Treatment Plant. (*GWN 282*)

Duncans Creek School 1921-22, *left to right,* first row, kneeling: Delia Puckett, Mildred Maudlin, Grace Hammet, Dessie Holman, Annie Lee Bradford, ———, ———, Lottie Tuggle, ——— Bradford, Ray Mauldin, Clyde Waycaster, ———, ———, Bob Burel, ——— Luther, Elmon Harrison, Otis Fagin, ———, Jessie Patrick, Carroll Puckett, ———, Auther Sloan. 2nd row: Viola Garner, Dollie Mae Capps, Selmer Maudlin, Lucille Cain, Tiny Tuggle, Ora Rolin, Estelle Barnett, Eva Waycaster, Lula Fagin, Lena Lois Cronic, Ella Crenshaw, Ila Mae Garner, Rosa Williams, Lucille Roebuck, Tennie Bradford, Clara Mae Sloan, Vera Harrison, Lola Patrick, Mae Holman, Ruth Tuggle, ——— Holman, Capoline Mauldin, Dewey Holman, Clint Roebuck, ———, Garnet Etheridge, ———; 3rd row: Clifford Davis, Lawsha Mauldin, Carl Patrick, Cline Ethridge, Ross Boggs, Bliss Mauldin, Curtis Rolin, Clarence Williams, Frank Mauldin, Claude Crenshaw, Gaines Davis, Ross Burel, Avery Waycaster, Thomas Roebuck, Wesley Daniel, ———, Troy Holman, ———, Crawford Puckett, ———, Huey Harrison, ——— Hammet, Willie Bradford, Milton Burel, Garland Ethridge. Teachers: Esther Mauldin, Gwendolyn Mann and Rev. Floyd Hendricks. *(GWN 89)*

Glover School was on Rockbridge Road, now Jimmy Carter Boulevard, Norcross, when this 1920s photograph was made. The building which replaced this one that burned in 1932 became home to Glover Baptist Church when this school was consolidated with others in the area. (*Photo from Nolan D. Singleton*)

The students of Pleasant Hill Academy were caught by the photographer on August 12, 1897. Instructors were Dr. Aubrey S. Hopkins and E. T. "Zeke" Hopkins. Notice baseball bat for discipline or play leaning on table that holds Bible. (*GWN 263*)

The 1914 Graduating Class of Dacula High School pose in front of the school built in 1910. This brick two-story building with a cupola on the roof replaced a wooden school built in 1892, and it burned in 1944, one month before graduation. First row: Mr. J. B. Brookshire, Annie Mae Hinton, Effie Sikes, Bessie Freeman, Ollie Mae Pharr. Second row: Cassie Tanner, Snowdell Wood, Odessa Tanner, Ruby Wood. Third row: Hugh Hood, _____, Willie Hall, Otis Newton Pharr, Joe Rice. (*GWN 127*)

The Union School on Stone Mountain-Lilburn Rd., c. 1914.
Teachers were Vada Nash Johnson and Bertha Brooks (GWN 13)

Younger children at Beaver Ruin Academy display the *c.* 1911 fad: hoops. Front, kneeling: 3rd from left, Ivah McDaniel (m. Allison), 7th from left, Willie Lee Mills (m. Bill Vaughan), next, Dewey Warbington, next, Mary B. Mills (m. Victor Bolton) girl in hoop; 2nd row, last on right: Jessie B. Bolton (m. Joseph Pickens); 3rd row, 1st: Clarence Warbington, 4th from left, teacher Alma Craig (m. John Minor), 5th from left, Edna Mills (m. Mitcham) and 6th from left, Chloe Martin (m. Homer Humphries). *(GWN 60)*

Glenn School, Rockbridge Road between U. S. 78 and Centerville, in 1909. Teachers, Miss Stacy and Miss Mobley must have had rough time with students as four of them have escaped onto the roof. *(GWN 73)*

171

Pharr Academy near Snellville had Hoyt P. Oliver for teacher in this 1910 photograph. *(GWN 222)*

Old Suwanee School students pose in 1901. Mrs. Eula Dillard, back row center, was teacher. Notice some boys wear buttons on their chests and older girls (plus last boy right rear) have ribbon corsages. Two black-hatted boys hold open books. *(GWN 116)*

Harris Academy commencement exercises or other activity with audience observing in 1900. Note Leg-of-mutton sleeves and bonnets on ladies in audience and the backwards "N" on the banner. (*GWN 299*)

Bertie Sigman taught Peachtree School in this 1911 group. *Left to right*, first row: Ural Graham, Enoch Johnson, Alfonzo Teagle, Gordon Bradford, Clyd Crumbley, Eula Braziel, Inez McDonald, Louis Brandford, Sallie Stevenson, Gertrude Stevenson, Erman Mosley, Clarence Cantrell, Hoyt Braziel, Clarence O'Kelly, Kline McDonald, _____, and Willie Graham. 2nd row: Arthur Nelson, Manda Davis, Abe Crumbley, and Bertha Bradford. 3rd row: _____, Sallie Crumbley, Louis Davis, Blanche Brandford, Ethel Brandford, Carrie Braziel, Mat Davis, Lou Mosley, and Bert Davis. 4th row: _____Nelson, Mamie McDonald, Clifford Davis, _____, Andrew Johnson, Clifford Johnson, John Mosley, Earl Davis, Creighton Braziel, Jack Mosley, Otis Teagle, Tom McDonald, Major Cantrell (holding baby), and Charlie Tullis. Peachtree School was consolidated with others in the area in 1930 to form Sunny Hill School which served the area until further consolidation in the 1950s, took that school out of existence. (*GWN 15*)

Carter's Academy students c. 1900, Bay Creek district. A reminder of the "brush arbor" schools of early Gwinnett are these students of James Albert Augustus Smith who posed on the grounds near the one-room schoolhouse that still had no well or toilet by 1923. (*Photo from Evelyn Green*)

The 1922 students, grades 1-7, of Jackson Academy, built in early 1900s on land donated by Andrew Cary Jackson, on today's Sever Road. Term was 7 months and students sat at double desks, brought own tin cups for water and used nearby woods for toilet facilities. *Left to right,* top row: Hubert Davis, Maebell Chadwick, Virgie Atkinson, Lois Cooper, Nora Hamilton, (teacher), Florence Atkinson and Fellie Parks; third row: Andrew Thompson, Oliver Moon, Irwin Huff, Clifford Thompson, Roy Thompson, Grady Parks, F.C. Davis, John Jackson and Thomas Chadwick; second row, seated: Louise Thompson, Ruth Chadwick, Kelly Adams, Mattie Bell Davis, Florine Spivey, Mildred Davis and Alvin Thompson; front seated: Carl Thompson, Thurman Huff, Jack Moon (?), John Thompson, Gerald Huff, Noel Johnson, Cliff West, Arnold Huff, and Otis Thompson. (GWN 339)

AT LEISURE

No matter how hard working, the individual has always had some leisure time with which a creative mind can always find ways to enjoy. Pleasures might vary from a plug of tobacco or a stick to whittle to an extended vacation. In the agrarian society, Saturday was the traditional day to go to town for the necessities not produced on the farm. Sundays were reserved for attending church services and visiting with relatives for Sunday dinner. Family reunions were held at home or at church and relatives came from far and wide bringing all sorts of delightful foods with them. There were organized picnics at churches and factories, and sometimes groups went to Stone Mountain or to Grant Park in Atlanta.

From the time of the Indians, the fields and forests of Gwinnett had abundant animal life attractive to hunters: coon, deer, quail, dove, opossum, squirrel and rabbit. Ponds, lakes and streams supplied bream, bass, catfish and turtles. Hunting, frog-gigging, catching turtles called "turkle-grabbling," and fishing provided food for the table as well as enjoyment to sportsmen.

Music has always been a part of the pastimes of Gwinnett. At one time, most towns had a bandstand on the square where local groups performed on Saturdays and Sundays and the brass band was popular around the turn of the century. Dancing was enjoyed by the young but specific rules in the Baptist decorum specifically forbade dancing so many young Baptists got around this rule by playing a game called "twistification," which was almost dancing.

Many participated in or observed parades, political rallies, demonstrations and baseball games. Some passed the afternoon watching or playing checkers in the shade of the town square with homemade board and bottle caps for checks. Two cities had movie theaters: the Strand and Thompson in Lawrenceville, and the Capes and Allen theaters in Buford. In the 1920s radio came into Gwinnett homes bringing hours of entertainment and news. Some housewives became involved with soap operas: "Stella Dallas" and "Pepper Young's Family." Television entered our lives in 1948 when WSB-TV began broadcasting from Atlanta; quickly followed by WAGA-TV and WLWA-TV. Only the automobile has had more impact than television on Gwinnett lives.

Organizations and societies took up a portion of our free time. Groups who have met or still meet include the Sons and Daughters of Confederate Veterans, Odd

GENESCO employees enjoy a square dance to Roger Furlong's band in Lawrenceville High School gym about 1950. Plant manager Herbert Corley (center left, with woman in bolero dress) can be seen. Also spotted there were Lewis Holcombe, Tom and Mary Davis, Richard Taylor and Hugh "Bud" Hipp, foreman, (center, rear, with hand on chin). *(GWN 295)*

Fellows, Knights of Pythias, Woodmen of The World, The Farmers' Alliance, The Masons, Order of the Eastern Star, The American Legion, Veterans of Foreign Wars, Junior Chamber of Commerce, Rotary, Lions, Kiwanis, Pilot Club, Sons, Daughters, and Children of the American Revolution, and the Gwinnett Historical Society, established in 1966.

Strickland Springs, a flag station on what became the Southern Railroad, at present Buford Highway between Duluth and Suwanee, was a resort in earlier years when folks in Atlanta took the train out, sometimes staying at the Wood Hotel, to enjoy the mineral waters which were considered beneficial. Those captured on this c. 1910 photograph are, seated, *left to right*: Stevie Brogdon, Brock Edmondson, Stell Harris, Marvin B. Verner, Viola Bennett, _____ Norton, Ross Johnston, Mabry Verner. Standing: Annie Lee Baxter, Marcus Mashburn, Winnie Little, Carfax Baxter, Hal Rhodes, Fannie Lou Patillo, Covert Harris, Villa Rhodes, Roy E. Johnson, and Clara Bennett. (*GWN 121*)

Brass bands were popular in the early years of this century as this local group met for practice in 1910. *(GWN 142)*

The Dacula Brass Band donned their uniforms for a performance in 1909. Seated, *left to right:* Jim Wilson, Samuel Herbert Hinton, ———, Beverly Ambrose and Edsel Pharr; 2nd row: Otha Pharr, Ben Wilson, Frank McMillian, J. C. "Jim" Pool, Otis Pharr and Frank Pharr; back row: Guy Sammons (?), Henry Stanley, Hovey Pharr, Al McMillian, Hugh Hood and Royce Pharr. *(GWN 148)*

183

Three separate pastimes are shown in this Buford photo from the 1920s: the brass band; a demonstration march; and the skating rink seen in center background at the site of the Big Spring. The photographer stood at Moreno Street and aimed the camera down unpaved Alexander Street at left. Brick house at the corner of Alexander and Park Streets was absorbed into the City Barn Complex that was constructed in the early 1950s when the spring was covered over and the waters carried away by culverts. (*GWN 133*)

184

Community picnic, c. 1900, was held in the pasture of John A.Minor, near today's intersection of Beaver Ruin Road and I-85. Creek in edge of woods at left rear of photograph is location where a bridge was built in 1984 where Shackelford Road crosses Bromolow Creek. (*GWN 62*)

Buford baseball team, 1908, in front of fence with "Brown and Roberts ice cold drinks" sign. Caps have "B" for Buford. *Left to right,* front: Bonnie Stringer, Belva Power, Ned Brogdon, Sam Chapman and George Brogdon; back row: Howard Sudderth, Clyde W. Power, Arch Holland, Hubert Power, Simon Allen, Vic Allen, John Allen and Roy Wilson. *(GWN 361-83)*

Lawrenceville baseball team 1913. Bat boy, Lewis Powell; seated, *left to right:* ———, ———, Rob Brown, Chalmers W. Powell, ———, Mr. Brown, Grover C. Montgomery, behind bats, Oliver Russell Juhan, Bob Robinson, George Bagwell; standing, *left to right:* Jack Poe, Tyler Peeples, Lyle Williams, ———, Tom Webb, Charlie McConnell, Col. I. L. Oakes, Will McGee, Col. O. A. Nix, A. T. Green, E. "Samp" Garner, ——— Brannon and Awtry Webb. *(GWN 273)*

The children can hardly wait for the photographer to get done to they can begin dinner at the Joel Abner Turner family reunion on New Hope Road in 1906. Besides Joel and wife, Estelle Robinson, and their offspring, there were also the families of Joel's brothers Daniel and Henry Turner. *(GWN 298)*

Left: Most of the residents of Five Forks attended the Nash and Stancil family reunion at the Nash homeplace on River Road in 1920. *(GWN 108)*

Miss Mattie Wages and J. Fletcher
Puckett are caught on film while on a
Sunday afternoon drive in 1919, the year
before they were married. *(GWN 95)*

At right: Allen Theatre, Buford, showed Walt Disney's "Old Yeller" in 1956
and then closed for good. Happiness, indeed, cost little: double feature and
cartoon on Saturday cost seventeen cents. Door at far right was the colored
entrance and led directly to the balcony. *(Photo from Billy Cain)*

Allen C. Daniel enjoys his tobacco and the joys of a rocking chair on the front porch. His cane rests on his knees. (*GWN 223*)

Opposite; Hotel guests gather on the ornate porch of the Medlock House, Thrasher Street, Norcross, in 1888. They had probably come up from Atlanta on the "Airline Belle" to enjoy the fresh air. The hotel was built by R. O. Medlock, later became a private home, and is now demolished. The shutters were closed to protect the draperies from fading from the sun. (*GWN 271*)

194

Employees of Bona Allen Shoe Factory enjoy their annual watermelon cutting held at Pass's Lake near Buford in the 1930s. *(GWN 132)*

Emory Chatham operates an elaborate fountain in drug store in Buford. Even in 1901 things went better with Coca Cola. *(GWN 184)*

At left: S. J. Puckett and friend display their catch in 1918, *(GWN 155)* and *at right:* two hunters display a catch of another kind in front of the Buford depot. Lantern for night hunting and chains on tires for hunting in woods were a necessity as was the possum dog. Possums were not killed but were caught and fed until fattened and the scavengers' insides were cleaned out and then they were cooked with sweet potatoes. *(Photo from Robert Saine)*

The "Goatman" was the title used by Chess McCartney on his journeys from Florida to Maine for over thirty years. The goatman's passing through town or countryside was reason to drop everything and see the wondrous sight of his steel-wheeled wagon piled high with all manner of junk and pulled by a herd of goats. The unkempt McCartney was minister of the Free Thinking Christian Mission outside of Jeffersonville, Georgia, where he sometimes lived in an abandoned school bus. (*Photo from Louise Burton*)

Mrs. Lula Kent Block and her husband are photographed enroute to vacation in Florida in 1915. The bridge was one lane with wider places, seen here, for meeting traffic. The Blocks were turning around because a portion of the bridge was flooded and they had to wait until the water subsided before they continued their journey. (*GWN 65*)

Buford area Confederate Veterans including Dr. Powers, Fred Sears, Jeff and Mose Pass, and David H. Puckett were photographed with others in the early years of the century. (GWN 141)

Odd Fellows of Buford at dinner meeting c. 1900 (GWN 140)

BIBLIOGRAPHY

Bonner, James C., *The Georgia Story,* Harlow Publishing Co., Oklahoma City, OK, 1961.

Flanigan, J. C., *Gwinnett Churches,* 1911.

Flanigan, J. C., *History of Gwinnett County, Georgia, Vol. I,* Tyler & Co., Hapeville, GA, 1943.

Flanigan, James C., *History of Gwinnett County, Georgia, Vol. II,* Longino & Porter, Inc., Hapeville, GA, 1959.

Garrett, Franklin M., *Atlanta and Environs,* University of Georgia Press, Atlanta, GA, 1954.

Garrett, Franklin M., *Yesterday's Atlanta,* E. A. Seeman Publishing Co., Miami, FL, 1974.

Hutchins, Myldred, *The History of Carl and Auburn,* CHB Printing and Binding, Lakemont, GA, 1981.

Konter, Sherry, *Vanishing Georgia,* University of Georgia Press, Athens, GA, 1982.

McCabe, Alice Smythe, *Gwinnett County, Georgia, Families 1818-1968,* Cherokee Publishing Co., Atlanta, GA, 1980.

Wynn, Bob, *Gwinnett Daily News,* several historical articles.

NAME INDEX

SUBJECT INDEX